LEARNING ABOUT
Animals

Catherine Veitch

Raintree

Chicago, Illinois

The author would like to dedicate this book to her mother,
Jacqueline Veitch, who inspired her with a love of nature.

© 2014 Raintree
an imprint of Capstone Global Library, LLC
Chicago, Illinois
capstonepub.com

Edited by Dan Nunn, Rebecca Rissman,
and Sian Smith
Designed by Joanna Hinton-Malivoire
Picture research by Mica Brancic
Production by Sophia Argyris
Originated by Capstone Global Library Ltd

Library of Congress Cataloging-in-Publication Data
Veitch, Catherine.
Learning about animals / Catherine Veitch.
pages cm.—(The natural world)
 Includes bibliographical references and index.
ISBN 978-1-4109-5404-6 (hardback)
ISBN 978-1-4109-5409-1 (paperback)
1. Animals—Juvenile literature. I. Title.
 QL49.V368 2014

 590—dc23   2012049395

Image Credits

Alamy: Avico Ltd, 18, 23; Avalon: NHPA/Stephen
Dalton, 16, 24; Shutterstock: Anthony Shaw
Photography, cover, Cathy Keifer, 6, 22, Christian
Mueller, 17, Dmitry Kalinovsky, 12, Eduard Kyslynskyy,
15, Frantisek Czanner, 19, Herbert Kratky, 13, Irina
Tischenko, 11, 22, 23, kool99, 12, 23, Mary Lane, 20
(inset), Mogens Trolle, 21, 23, PaulShlykov, 5 (inset),
Peter Krejzl, 9, 22, REDSTARSTUDIO, 5, Reinhold
Leitner, 20, 24, Sarel, back cover, 7, Sebastian Duda,
14 (all), 24, sergioboccardo, 21 (inset), Volodymyr
Burdiak, 10, 22, Whytock, 4, worldswildlifewonders,
8, 23

We would like to thank Michael Bright for his
invaluable help in the preparation of this book.

Every effort has been made to contact copyright
holders of any material reproduced in this book.
Any omissions will be rectified in subsequent
printings if notice is given to the publisher.

Contents

Anteater

nose

tail

4

Cat

claw

whiskers

5

Chameleon

crest

toes

6

Crab

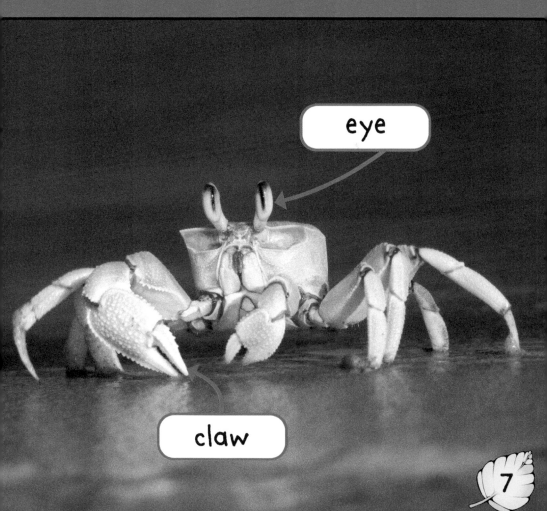

eye

claw

Crocodile

snout

tooth

scales

8

Deer

antlers

ear

Duck

tail

beak

Fish

fin

gill

fin

Goat

horn

hoof

beard

Hare

ear

foot

Hedgehog

spines

snout

14

Mouse

paw

whiskers

Owl

wing

talon

Robin

beak

leg

17

Sheep

horn

woolly coat

Squirrel

tail

whiskers

Tortoise

claws

shell

mouth

Zebra

mane

hoof

Picture Glossary

 **antlers** hard parts on an animal's head that look like branches. Animals can use antlers to fight or protect themselves.

 **beak** hard part of a bird's mouth. Beaks can be different shapes, and they are used to help birds eat.

 **crest** skin or feathers that stick up on top of an animal's head

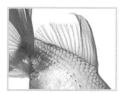 **fin** part of a fish that helps the fish move through the water

 **gill** part of a fish that helps the fish breathe

 **hoof** hard part of the foot of some animals. Horses and goats have hooves.

 **horn** hard, pointed part that grows out of an animal's head. Sheep and goats have horns.

 **mane** hair that grows on the necks of animals such as zebras, horses, or lions

 **scales** small, hard, overlapping parts that cover the skin of fish and reptiles

 **shell** a hard body covering. Many animals with shells can hide inside them so that other animals cannot hurt them.

 **snout** mouth and nose of some animals. A hedgehog has a snout.

 **spines** stiff spikes. Spines can help keep animals safe from other animals that want to eat them.

 **talon** long, sharp, hooked claw on the foot of an eagle or another bird. Talons are used to catch and carry things.

Notes for Parents and Teachers

- Go on a trip to a zoo. Take this book along, and ask the children to spot some of the animals shown in the book. Encourage the children to sketch or photograph what they see. Can they label the animals and animal parts?
- Use the images and labels to make a class book. Discuss the body parts of different animals and what the animals might use them for.